Rum & Yum

40 Trendy, Savory and Sweet Recipes
for the Modern Cook

LPS Publishing House LLC

Contents

INTRODUCTION

Rum isn't just for cocktails, it's a bold, flavorful ingredient that can transform everyday recipes into something unforgettable. In this cookbook, you'll find 40 carefully crafted recipes that highlight how a single bottle of rum can add depth, warmth, and character to sweet and savory dishes alike.

Inside, you'll get clear, step-by-step instructions for a wide range of recipes, including main dishes, side dishes, desserts, and drinks, all featuring rum in a meaningful way. Whether it's rum-glazed chicken, caramelized plantains, a rich rum cake, or a refreshing fruit-forward cocktail, each recipe has been developed with flavor, balance, and ease in mind.

The ingredients are simple. The methods are straightforward. And the results? Packed with taste and perfect for any occasion — from casual weeknight meals to entertaining guests.

If you're looking to cook with confidence and creativity, Cook with a Splash of Rum is your go-to guide. Open the bottle, follow the steps, and bring a touch of spirit to every bite.

Main Dishes

Jerk Glazed Chicken Thighs

INGREDIENTS

4 bone-in chicken thighs
2 tbsp dark rum
1 tbsp olive oil
1 tbsp soy sauce
1 tbsp brown sugar
1 tsp allspice
½ tsp black pepper
½ tsp salt
Juice of ½ lime
1 tsp dried thyme
1 clove garlic, minced
2 green onions, chopped

4
SERVINGS

15 MINS
PREP TIME

25 MINS
COOK TIME

INSTRUCTIONS

1. Combine rum, one tbsp oil, soy sauce, brown sugar, allspice, black pepper, salt, lime juice, thyme, garlic, and green onions in a deep-bottom bowl.
2. Add chicken thighs and coat well. Cover and marinate in a cool place for 2 to 4 hours.
3. Preheat grill on moderate heat and lightly oil the grates.
4. Place the meat skin-side down and grill for 5–6 minutes on one side until cooked through.
5. Brush with leftover marinade during the last few minutes (make sure to boil the marinade first for safety).
6. Let it sit for 5 minutes before serving.

NUTRITIONAL VALUES (PER SERVING):

Calories: 330 | Protein: 27g | Carbs: 7g | Fat: 20g

BBQ Pulled Pork Sandwiches

INGREDIENTS

2 lbs pork shoulder
½ cup dark rum
1 cup BBQ sauce
1 tbsp brown sugar
1 tsp smoked paprika
1 tsp garlic powder
½ tsp salt
½ tsp black pepper
6 sandwich buns

4
SERVINGS

15 MINS
PREP TIME

6 Hours
COOK TIME

INSTRUCTIONS

1. Pat the pork shoulder dry and massage it with smoked paprika, garlic powder, salt, and crushed pepper.
2. Grab the shallow bowl and mix BBQ sauce, rum, and brown sugar until combined.
3. Place the pork in a slow cooker and ladle the sauce over it.
4. Cover and cook on low for 6-7 hours until the pork is very tender.
5. Shred the meat using two forks directly in the slow cooker, then toss in the cooking juices.
6. Lightly toast the buns and fill each with the pulled pork. Serve hot, accompanied by optional slaw or pickles.

NUTRITIONAL VALUES (PER SERVING):

Calories: 410 | Protein: 32g | Carbs: 28g | Fat: 18g

Garlic Shrimp Skillet

INGREDIENTS

1 lb large shrimp, peeled
2 tbsp dark rum
1 tbsp olive oil
3 cloves garlic, minced
½ tsp salt
¼ tsp red pepper flakes
Juice of ½ lemon
Chopped parsley to finish

4
SERVINGS

10 MINS
PREP TIME

5 MINS
COOK TIME

INSTRUCTIONS

1. Rinse and pat the shrimp dry.
2. Heat one tbsp oil in a skillet on moderate heat, then toss in the garlic and red pepper flakes.
3. Cook for 30 seconds until the garlic gets fragrant but not browned.
4. Add shrimp and cook for 2 more minutes, stirring occasionally.
5. Ladle in the rum and lemon juice and let the shrimp simmer for another 3 to 4 minutes until pink and firm.
6. Garnish with parsley and serve immediately.

NUTRITIONAL VALUES (PER SERVING):

Calories: 220 | Protein: 25g | Carbs: 2g | Fat: 11g

Beef Stir-Fry with Rum Sauce

INGREDIENTS

1 lb flank steak, sliced thin

3 tbsp dark rum

2 tbsp soy sauce

1 tbsp brown sugar

1 tbsp vegetable oil

1 tsp cornstarch

1 bell pepper, sliced

½ onion, sliced

1 clove garlic, minced

4
SERVINGS

15 MINS
PREP TIME

15 MINS
COOK TIME

INSTRUCTIONS

1. In a small, deep-bottom bowl, whisk together rum, soy sauce, brown sugar, and cornstarch.
2. Heat one tbsp oil in a skillet or wok on moderate-high heat.
3. Add the meat slices and cook for 3 to 4 minutes, until just browned. Then, remove and set aside.
4. Add mashed garlic, bell pepper, and onion to the pan and stir-fry for 2-3 minutes.
5. Return the beef to the pan, ladle in the sauce, and toss everything together.
6. Let it cook for another 3 to 4 minutes until the sauce thickens. Serve hot.

NUTRITIONAL VALUES (PER SERVING):

Calories: 360 | Protein: 28g | Carbs: 10g | Fat: 22g

Skirt Steak Fajitas

INGREDIENTS

1½ lbs skirt steak

2 tbsp dark rum

1 tbsp lime juice

1 tbsp olive oil

1 tsp chili powder

½ tsp salt

½ tsp cumin

1 red bell pepper, sliced

1 onion, sliced

8 small tortillas

4
SERVINGS

15 MINS
PREP TIME

10 MINS
COOK TIME

INSTRUCTIONS

1. Grab the shallow bowl and combine rum, lime juice, one tbsp oil, chili powder, cumin, and salt.
2. Add steak to the marinade and coat well. Refrigerate for 1 hour. Preheat a grill pan or skillet on moderate heat.
3. Grill steak for 3-4 minutes on one side, then let it rest for 5 minutes. Slice the steak thinly against the grain.
4. Sauté bell pepper and onion in the same pan until tender. Warm tortillas and fill with steak and sautéed veggies. Serve warm.

NUTRITIONAL VALUES (PER SERVING):

Calories: 430 | Protein: 30g | Carbs: 24g | Fat: 24g

Braised Chicken Thighs – Island Style

INGREDIENTS

4 bone-in chicken thighs
¼ cup dark rum
1 cup chicken broth
1 tbsp tomato paste
1 tbsp oil
1 tsp allspice
½ tsp salt
1 clove garlic, minced
½ onion, diced
1 small tomato, chopped

4
SERVINGS

10 MINS
PREP TIME

45 MINS
COOK TIME

INSTRUCTIONS

1. Heat one tbsp oil in a pot on moderate heat.
2. Brown the chicken thighs on both sides for 4 to 5 minutes on one side. Remove and set aside.
3. Use the same pot and sauté the onion, garlic, and tomato for 2 minutes.
4. Toss in allspice and tomato paste and cook for 1 more minute.
5. Add rum to deglaze the pot, then ladle in chicken broth and get it to a gentle simmer.
6. Return the chicken to the cover and cook for 35 to 40 minutes or until tender. Serve hot.

NUTRITIONAL VALUES (PER SERVING):

Calories: 380 | Protein: 29g | Carbs: 6g | Fat: 26g

Salmon with Pineapple Salsa

INGREDIENTS

4 salmon fillets (skin on)

3 tbsp dark rum

1 tbsp olive oil

1 tbsp lime juice

1 garlic clove, minced

Salt and black pepper to taste

1 cup diced pineapple

¼ cup red onion, finely chopped

1 small red chili, minced (optional)

1 tbsp fresh cilantro, chopped

4 SERVINGS

15 MINS PREP TIME

12 MINS COOK TIME

INSTRUCTIONS

1. In a small deep-bottom bowl, mix rum, one tbsp oil, lime juice, garlic, salt, and black pepper.
2. Place the salmon fillets in a dish and brush with the rum mixture. Let sit for 15 minutes.
3. Meanwhile, make the salsa by combining pineapple, red onion, chili, and cilantro. Set aside.
4. Heat a grill pan or outdoor grill on moderate heat.
5. Place salmon skin-side down and grill for 5 to 6 minutes, then flip and cook 4 to 5 minutes more, basting with the remaining marinade.
6. Serve topped with fresh pineapple salsa.

NUTRITIONAL VALUES (PER SERVING):

Calories: 340 | Protein: 30g | Carbs: 6g | Fat: 22g

Oven-Baked Chicken Wings

4	**10 MINS**	**45 MINS**
SERVINGS	PREP TIME	COOK TIME

INGREDIENTS

2 lbs chicken wings

3 tbsp dark rum

2 tbsp olive oil

1 tbsp smoked paprika

1 tsp garlic powder

½ tsp ground black pepper

½ tsp salt

INSTRUCTIONS

1. Preheat oven to 400°F (200°C). Arrange the baking tray with parchment paper.
2. Take the large shallow bowl and whisk together rum, two tbsp oil, paprika, garlic powder, pepper, and salt.
3. Add the wing meat and toss until well-coated.
4. Spread wings out on the tray in a single layer.
5. Bake for 43-45 minutes, turning once halfway through until golden and crisp.
6. Serve hot with dipping sauce or fresh lime wedges.

NUTRITIONAL VALUES (PER SERVING):

Calories: 390 | Protein: 32g | Carbs: 1g | Fat: 28g

Herb-Crusted Pork Tenderloin

INGREDIENTS

1½ lbs pork tenderloin
3 tbsp dark rum
1 tbsp olive oil
1 tsp dried rosemary
1 tsp dried thyme
1 tsp garlic powder
½ tsp salt
½ tsp black pepper

4
SERVINGS

15 MINS
PREP TIME

30 MINS
COOK TIME

INSTRUCTIONS

1. Preheat oven to 375°F (190°C).
2. In a small deep-bottom bowl, combine rum, one tbsp oil, rosemary, thyme, garlic powder, salt, and crushed pepper.
3. Rub the mixture all over the tenderloin meat and place it in a roasting dish.
4. Roast for 25 to 30 minutes or until internal temperature reaches 145°F (63°C).
5. Put the pork aside to rest for 5 minutes before slicing into medallions.
6. Serve with roasted vegetables or mashed cauliflower.

NUTRITIONAL VALUES (PER SERVING):

Calories: 300 | Protein: 33g | Carbs: 1g | Fat: 18g

Coconut Curry Shrimp

INGREDIENTS

1 lb shrimp, peeled and deveined

2 tbsp dark rum

1 cup coconut milk

1 tbsp olive oil

1 tbsp curry powder

1 garlic clove, minced

½ onion, diced

Salt and pepper to taste

4
SERVINGS

10 MINS
PREP TIME

15 MINS
COOK TIME

INSTRUCTIONS

1. Heat one tbsp oil in a skillet on moderate heat and sauté onion and garlic for 2 minutes.
2. Add shrimp and cook for 2-3 minutes until they begin to turn pink.
3. Sprinkle in curry powder and toss well.
4. Ladle in coconut milk and rum, and get the sauce to a simmer.
5. Let it cook gently for 6 to 8 minutes until the shrimp are done properly and the sauce has thickened slightly.
6. Serve hot over steamed rice or cauliflower rice.

NUTRITIONAL VALUES (PER SERVING):

Calories: 330 | Protein: 27g | Carbs: 4g | Fat: 22g

Teriyaki Chicken Kebabs

INGREDIENTS

1½ lbs chicken breast, cubed

¼ cup dark rum

2 tbsp soy sauce

1 tbsp honey

1 tbsp olive oil

1 garlic clove, minced

1 tsp grated ginger

1 bell pepper, cubed

1 red onion, cut into chunks

Wooden or metal skewers

4
SERVINGS

20 MINS
PREP TIME

12 MINS
COOK TIME

INSTRUCTIONS

1. Grab the shallow bowl and combine rum, soy sauce, honey, oil, garlic, and ginger.
2. Add chicken cubes and marinate for 1 hour (at least) in the refrigerator.
3. Thread chicken, bell pepper, and onion alternately onto skewers.
4. Preheat grill or grill pan on moderate heat and lightly oil the surface.
5. Cook kebabs for 10 to 12 minutes, turning occasionally and brushing with leftover marinade.
6. Serve warm with rice or salad.

NUTRITIONAL VALUES (PER SERVING):

Calories: 350 | Protein: 32g | Carbs: 8g | Fat: 20g

Spiced Meatball Skillet

INGREDIENTS

1 lb ground beef or lamb

2 tbsp dark rum

1 egg

¼ cup almond flour or breadcrumbs

1 tsp allspice

1 tsp garlic powder

½ tsp salt

½ tsp black pepper

1 tbsp olive oil

½ cup broth or water

4
SERVINGS

15 MINS
PREP TIME

20 MINS
COOK TIME

INSTRUCTIONS

1. In a deep-bottom bowl, combine ground meat, egg, almond flour, allspice, garlic powder, salt, and crushed pepper. Mix until just combined.
2. Shape the meat into small meatballs, approximately 1 inch in diameter.
3. Heat one tbsp oil in a skillet on moderate heat and brown meatballs on all sides for about 6 to 8 minutes.
4. Add rum and broth to the pan, lower the heat, and cover.
5. Simmer for 10 minutes, letting the meatballs absorb the flavors and cook through.
6. Serve with mashed root veggies or rice.

NUTRITIONAL VALUES (PER SERVING):

Calories: 380 | Protein: 30g | Carbs: 3g | Fat: 26g

Side Dishes

Roasted Sweet Potatoes with Rum Butter

INGREDIENTS

3 medium sweet potatoes, peeled and cubed
3 tbsp unsalted butter
2 tbsp dark rum
1 tbsp olive oil
½ tsp cinnamon
¼ tsp salt
Black pepper to taste

4 SERVINGS   **10 MINS** PREP TIME   **35 MINS** COOK TIME

INSTRUCTIONS

1. Preheat oven to 400°F (200°C). Arrange the baking tray with parchment paper.
2. In a small saucepan, melt the butter over low heat, then toss in the rum and cinnamon. Set aside.
3. Grab the shallow bowl and toss sweet potato cubes with one tbsp oil, salt, and black pepper.
4. Spread the potatoes on the tray and roast for 25 minutes.
5. Remove the tray and drizzle with the rum butter mixture.
6. Return the dish to the oven and roast for an additional 8-10 minutes.

NUTRITIONAL VALUES (PER SERVING):

Calories: 210 | Protein: 2g | Carbs: 27g | Fat: 10g

Grilled Pineapple Slices with Rum Glaze

INGREDIENTS

1 fresh pineapple, peeled and sliced into rings
2 tbsp dark rum
1 tbsp maple syrup
1 tbsp melted butter
½ tsp cinnamon
Pinch of salt

4
SERVINGS

10 MINS
PREP TIME

10 MINS
COOK TIME

INSTRUCTIONS

1. In a small, deep-bottom bowl, whisk together rum, maple syrup, melted butter, cinnamon, and salt.
2. Preheat a grill or grill pan on moderate heat.
3. Brush both sides of the fruit rings with the glaze.
4. Grill for 4 to 5 minutes on one side until nicely charred and tender.
5. Brush with extra glaze before serving for extra shine and flavor.

NUTRITIONAL VALUES (PER SERVING):

Calories: 120 | Protein: 1g | Carbs: 20g | Fat: 4g

Caramelized Plantains with Spiced Rum

INGREDIENTS

2 ripe plantains, sliced
diagonally
2 tbsp dark rum
1 tbsp brown sugar or honey
2 tbsp butter
¼ tsp ground cinnamon
Pinch of salt

4
SERVINGS

05 MINS
PREP TIME

10 MINS
COOK TIME

INSTRUCTIONS

1. Heat butter in a skillet on moderate heat until melted and foamy.
2. Add plantain slices and cook for 2 to 3 minutes on one side until golden.
3. Sprinkle in cinnamon and salt, then drizzle over the brown sugar and rum.
4. Reduce heat slightly and cook for another 3 minutes, spooning the sauce over the plantains.
5. Serve warm as a side or dessert-style treat.

NUTRITIONAL VALUES (PER SERVING):

Calories: 190 | Protein: 1g | Carbs: 25g | Fat: 9g

Baked Brussels Sprouts with Rum-Maple Glaze

INGREDIENTS

1 lb Brussels sprouts, halved

2 tbsp olive oil

1 tbsp dark rum

1 tbsp maple syrup

½ tsp garlic powder

¼ tsp salt

Black pepper to taste

4
SERVINGS

10 MINS
PREP TIME

10 MINS
COOK TIME

INSTRUCTIONS

1. Preheat oven to 400°F (200°C).
2. Take the large shallow bowl and toss Brussels sprouts with two tbsp oil, garlic powder, salt, and black pepper.
3. Spread them cut-side down on the paper-arranged baking sheet. Roast for 20 minutes, then remove the roast from the oven.
4. In a small deep-bottom bowl, mix rum and maple syrup, then drizzle it over the sprouts.
5. Return to the oven and roast for another 8 to 10 minutes until caramelized and crispy.

NUTRITIONAL VALUES (PER SERVING):

Calories: 160 | Protein: 4g | Carbs: 14g | Fat: 10g

Braised Collard Greens

INGREDIENTS

1 bunch collard greens, stems removed and leaves chopped

2 tbsp dark rum

1 tbsp olive oil

2 cloves garlic, minced

½ small onion, diced

1 cup chicken or vegetable broth

¼ tsp red pepper flakes (optional)

Salt and black pepper to taste

4
SERVINGS

10 MINS
PREP TIME

35 MINS
COOK TIME

INSTRUCTIONS

1. Heat one tbsp oil in a large pot over moderate heat and sauté onion and garlic for 2 minutes.
2. Add chopped collard greens and toss until slightly wilted.
3. Ladle in the broth and rum, then add red pepper flakes, salt, and crushed pepper.
4. Get to a gentle simmer, cover, and cook for 30 minutes until greens are tender.
5. Remove the lid in the last few minutes to reduce excess liquid if needed. Serve warm.

NUTRITIONAL VALUES (PER SERVING):

Calories: 120 | Protein: 3g | Carbs: 8g | Fat: 8g

Baked Beans with Bacon and Rum

INGREDIENTS

2 cups cooked navy or pinto beans
4 slices bacon, chopped
¼ cup dark rum
½ cup tomato sauce
1 tbsp olive oil
1 small onion, diced
1 tbsp mustard
Salt and pepper to taste

4
SERVINGS

10 MINS
PREP TIME

45 MINS
COOK TIME

INSTRUCTIONS

1. Preheat oven to 375°F (190°C). In a skillet, cook chopped bacon until crisp, then transfer to a plate.
2. Use the same pan and sauté onion in bacon fat for 3 to 4 minutes. Add the rum and let it simmer for 1 minute to deglaze the pan.
3. Grab the shallow bowl and mix cooked beans, tomato sauce, mustard, onion mixture, and half of the bacon.
4. Transfer the mixture to the parchment paper-arranged baking dish and bake it uncovered for 35 minutes. Sprinkle with the remaining bacon and serve.

NUTRITIONAL VALUES (PER SERVING):

Calories: 260 | Protein: 11g | Carbs: 25g | Fat: 12g

Cornbread Muffins with Rum

INGREDIENTS

1 cup cornmeal
½ cup all-purpose flour
1 tbsp baking powder
½ tsp salt
1 egg
¾ cup milk
2 tbsp dark rum
2 tbsp melted butter or oil

4
SERVINGS

10 MINS
PREP TIME

20 MINS
COOK TIME

INSTRUCTIONS

1. Preheat oven to 375°F (190°C). Line a muffin tin. Grab the shallow bowl and combine cornmeal, flour, baking powder, and salt.
2. Take the other bowl and whisk together egg, milk, rum, and melted butter. Pour the wet elements mixture into the dry and stir just until combined.
3. Divide the batter equally into the muffin cups.
4. Bake for 16 to 18 minutes, or until tops are golden and a tooth-stick comes out clean.

NUTRITIONAL VALUES (PER SERVING):

Calories: 180 | Protein: 4g | Carbs: 23g | Fat: 7g

Skillet Mushrooms in Rum Cream Sauce

INGREDIENTS

2 cups sliced button or cremini mushrooms

2 tbsp dark rum

1 tbsp butter

1 tbsp olive oil

2 cloves garlic, minced

½ cup heavy cream

Salt and black pepper to taste

Fresh thyme or parsley for garnish

4
SERVINGS

10 MINS
PREP TIME

15 MINS
COOK TIME

INSTRUCTIONS

1. Heat one tbsp butter or oil in a skillet on moderate heat.
2. Add mushroom pieces and cook for 6-8 minutes, until they are browned and tender.
3. Add the mashed garlic and cook for 1 minute, until fragrant.
4. Ladle in the rum and simmer for 1 to 2 minutes to reduce slightly.
5. Add cream, then sprinkle with salt and crushed pepper, and let the sauce simmer for 4 to 5 minutes until thickened.
6. Garnish with fresh herbs and serve warm.

NUTRITIONAL VALUES (PER SERVING):

Calories: 230 | Protein: 4g | Carbs: 5g | Fat: 21g

Desserts

Classic Caribbean Rum Cake

INGREDIENTS

1½ cups all-purpose flour
1 cup butter, softened
4 eggs
¾ cup brown sugar
½ cup dark rum
1 tsp vanilla extract
1 tsp baking powder
½ tsp cinnamon
¼ tsp salt

10
SERVINGS

10 MINS
PREP TIME

20 MINS
COOK TIME

INSTRUCTIONS

1. Preheat oven to 350°F (175°C). Grease a bundt or loaf pan.
2. Cream butter with sugar until the texture gets fluffy, then mix in eggs, rum, and vanilla.
3. Take the other bowl and combine flour, baking powder, cinnamon powder, and salt.
4. Gradually stir in the dry ingredients (one at a time) into the wet mixture until smooth.
5. Ladle into the pan and bake for 50–55 minutes until a tooth-stick comes out clean.
6. Cool for 10 minutes, then invert and brush with extra rum if desired.

NUTRITIONAL VALUES (PER SERVING):

Calories: 360 | Protein: 5g | Carbs: 36g | Fat: 22g

Banana Bread with Toasted Walnuts

INGREDIENTS

3 ripe bananas, mashed
1½ cups flour
½ cup chopped toasted walnuts
2 eggs
½ cup melted butter
¼ cup dark rum
½ cup brown sugar
1 tsp baking soda
½ tsp cinnamon
Pinch of salt

8 SERVINGS **10 MINS** PREP TIME **55 MINS** COOK TIME

INSTRUCTIONS

1. Preheat oven to 350°F (175°C). Grease a loaf pan.
2. Mix mashed bananas with butter, eggs, sugar, and rum.
3. Take the other bowl, combine flour, baking soda, cinnamon, and salt.
4. Stir the dry ingredients (one at a time) into the wet elements mixture, then fold in the walnuts.
5. Pour batter into pan and bake 52–55 minutes until a tooth-stick comes out clean.
6. Cool for 10 minutes in a pan before transferring to a rack.

NUTRITIONAL VALUES (PER SERVING):

Calories: 310 | Protein: 5g | Carbs: 34g | Fat: 18g

Chocolate Brownies with Rum

INGREDIENTS

¾ cup unsalted butter
1 cup dark chocolate chips
2 eggs
½ cup brown sugar
¼ cup dark rum
½ cup flour
¼ cup cocoa powder
½ tsp baking powder
Pinch of salt

10
SERVINGS

10 MINS
PREP TIME

30 MINS
COOK TIME

INSTRUCTIONS

1. Preheat oven to 350°F (175°C). Line a square pan with parchment.
2. Melt the butter with the chocolate, then let it cool slightly.
3. Toss in eggs, brown sugar, and rum until smooth.
4. Mix flour, cocoa powder, baking powder, and salt, then fold into the batter.
5. Drop the mixture into the prepared pan and bake for 28–30 minutes or until the center is set.
6. Cool completely before slicing.

NUTRITIONAL VALUES (PER SERVING):

Calories: 290 | Protein: 4g | Carbs: 25g | Fat: 20g

Bread Pudding with Rum and Raisins

INGREDIENTS

5 cups cubed bread
2 cups milk
2 eggs
¼ cup dark rum
½ cup raisins
¼ cup melted butter
¼ cup brown sugar
1 tsp vanilla
½ tsp cinnamon
Pinch of salt

6
SERVINGS

15 MINS
PREP TIME

45 MINS
COOK TIME

INSTRUCTIONS

1. Preheat oven to 350°F (175°C). Grease a baking dish.
2. Soak raisins in rum for 10 minutes.
3. Grab the shallow bowl and whisk milk, eggs, sugar, vanilla, cinnamon, salt, and butter.
4. Add bread and raisins with rum; mix and let sit for 5 minutes.
5. Ladle the mixture into the dish and bake for 40–45 minutes, until golden and set.
6. Cool slightly before serving.

NUTRITIONAL VALUES (PER SERVING):

Calories: 330 | Protein: 7g | Carbs: 33g | Fat: 18g

Apple Fritters with Rum Glaze

INGREDIENTS

2 apples, diced
1 cup flour
1 tsp baking powder
½ tsp cinnamon
¼ tsp salt
2 tbsp brown sugar
1 egg
½ cup milk
2 tbsp dark rum
Oil for frying
Rum Glaze:
½ cup powdered sweetener
1 tbsp dark rum
1 tbsp milk

10
SERVINGS

10 MINS
PREP TIME

15 MINS
COOK TIME

INSTRUCTIONS

1. Mix flour, baking powder, cinnamon, salt, and sugar in a deep-bottom bowl.
2. Take the other bowl and whisk together the egg, milk, and rum. Then, combine this wet elements mixture with the dry ingredients.
3. Fold in apples to make a thick batter.
4. Heat one tbsp oil and fry spoonfuls of batter 2–3 minutes on one side until golden.
5. Drain and drizzle with glaze made by mixing glaze ingredients.
6. Serve warm.

NUTRITIONAL VALUES (PER SERVING):

Calories: 260 | Protein: 3g | Carbs: 30g | Fat: 14g

Baked Pears with Spiced Rum and Honey

INGREDIENTS

2 ripe pears, halved and cored
2 tbsp dark rum
2 tbsp honey
1 tbsp melted butter
½ tsp cinnamon
¼ tsp ground nutmeg

6
SERVINGS

10 MINS
PREP TIME

30 MINS
COOK TIME

INSTRUCTIONS

1. Preheat oven to 375°F (190°C). Place pear halves, cut side up, in the paper-arranged baking dish.
2. Grab the shallow bowl and mix rum, honey, butter, cinnamon, and nutmeg.
3. Spoon the mixture over each pear half generously.
4. Cover the dish with foil and bake for 18-20 minutes.
5. Uncover and bake for 10 more minutes until tender and lightly golden.
6. Serve warm with yogurt or any choice ice cream.

NUTRITIONAL VALUES (PER SERVING):

Calories: 180 | Protein: 1g | Carbs: 26g | Fat: 8g

Coconut Macaroons with Rum

INGREDIENTS

2 cups shredded unsweetened coconut
2 egg whites
¼ cup dark rum
¼ cup maple syrup or sweetener
½ tsp vanilla extract
Pinch of salt

10
SERVINGS

10 MINS
PREP TIME

20 MINS
COOK TIME

INSTRUCTIONS

1. Preheat oven to 325°F (165°C). Arrange the baking sheet with parchment paper.
2. Grab the shallow bowl and whisk the egg whites until they are slightly frothy.
3. Toss in rum, maple syrup, vanilla, and salt.
4. Add shredded coconut and mix until it is fully coated.
5. Scoop spoonfuls onto the baking sheet and shape into mounds.
6. Bake for 18–20 minutes until golden. Cool before serving.

NUTRITIONAL VALUES (PER SERVING):

Calories: 140 | Protein: 2g | Carbs: 10g | Fat: 10g

Fried Plantain Sundaes with Rum Sauce

INGREDIENTS

2 ripe plantains, sliced
2 tbsp butter
2 tbsp dark rum
2 tbsp maple syrup or honey
1 tsp cinnamon
Vanilla ice cream for serving

6
SERVINGS

10 MINS
PREP TIME

10 MINS
COOK TIME

INSTRUCTIONS

1. Heat butter in a skillet on moderate heat and add sliced plantains.
2. Fry for 3–4 minutes on one side until golden and tender.
3. In a small saucepan, warm rum, maple syrup, and cinnamon.
4. Simmer the sauce for 2 minutes or until it has slightly thickened.
5. Serve fried plantains in bowls with a scoop of ice cream.
6. Drizzle with warm rum sauce and serve immediately.

NUTRITIONAL VALUES (PER SERVING):

Calories: 290 | Protein: 2g | Carbs: 32g | Fat: 17g

Butter Pecan Cookies with Rum

INGREDIENTS

1 cup chopped pecans
½ cup butter, softened
¼ cup brown sugar
1 egg yolk
2 tbsp dark rum
1 cup flour
½ tsp vanilla extract
Pinch of salt

10
SERVINGS

10 MINS
PREP TIME

12 MINS
COOK TIME

INSTRUCTIONS

1. Preheat oven to 350°F (175°C). Arrange the baking sheet.
2. Cream the butter with sugar until it gets the smooth texture, then mix in the egg yolk, rum, and vanilla.
3. Toss in flour, salt, and chopped pecans to form a soft dough.
4. Roll into 1-inch balls and place on the baking sheet.
5. Flatten gently with your palm and bake for 10–12 minutes.
6. Cool completely before serving or storing.

NUTRITIONAL VALUES (PER SERVING):

Calories: 160 | Protein: 2g | Carbs: 12g | Fat: 12g

Grilled Peaches with Rum Caramel Drizzle

INGREDIENTS

2 ripe peaches, halved and pitted
1 tbsp olive oil
2 tbsp butter
2 tbsp dark rum
2 tbsp maple syrup or sweetener
Pinch of cinnamon

10
SERVINGS

10 MINS
PREP TIME

10 MINS
COOK TIME

INSTRUCTIONS

1. Preheat grill or grill pan and brush peach halves with olive oil.
2. Grill peaches cut-side face down for 3–4 minutes until lightly charred.
3. In a saucepan, melt the butter with add rum, maple syrup, and cinnamon.
4. Simmer for 2–3 minutes until slightly thickened.
5. Place grilled peaches on the serving platter and drizzle with warm rum caramel.
6. Serve with whipped cream or yogurt if desired.

NUTRITIONAL VALUES (PER SERVING):

Calories: 170 | Protein: 1g | Carbs: 19g | Fat: 10g

DRINKS

Classic Dark 'n' Stormy

INGREDIENTS

2 oz dark rum
4 oz ginger beer
½ oz fresh lime juice
Ice cubes
Lime wedge for garnish

1
SERVINGS

05 MINS
PREP TIME

INSTRUCTIONS

1. Fill a tall highball glass with fresh ice cubes to chill the base.
2. Ladle in the ginger beer, allowing it to settle halfway up the glass.
3. Add the fresh lime juice and let the flavors mix at the bottom.
4. Slowly float the dark rum over the top for a layered effect.
5. Garnish with a lime piece on the rim of the glass.
6. Stir gently if you prefer an even flavor before taking the first sip.

NUTRITIONAL VALUES (PER SERVING):

Calories: 130 | Protein: 0g | Carbs: 9g | Fat: 0g

Rum Mojito with Fresh Mint

INGREDIENTS

2 oz white rum

1 oz lime juice

6–8 fresh mint leaves

1 tsp honey or sweetener (optional)

Soda water

Ice cubes

1
SERVINGS

05 MINS
PREP TIME

INSTRUCTIONS

1. Place mint leaves with lime juice into a sturdy glass and gently crush them with the back of a spoon to release the oils.
2. Add the rum and sweetener (if using), then gently stir the mixture to combine.
3. Fill the glass with ice cubes, packing it to the top.
4. Slowly top off with soda water to add fizz and freshness.
5. Stir lightly with a spoon or straw to combine the flavors.
6. Garnish with mint leaves, using a sprig, and serve immediately for the best aroma.

NUTRITIONAL VALUES (PER SERVING):

Calories: 120 | Protein: 0g | Carbs: 5g | Fat: 0g

Pineapple Rum Punch

INGREDIENTS

4 oz pineapple juice
3 oz dark rum
1 oz orange juice
½ oz lime juice
Pineapple wedges and ice

2
SERVINGS

05 MINS
PREP TIME

INSTRUCTIONS

1. In a cocktail shaker, throw in pineapple juice, orange juice, lime juice, and dark rum.
2. Add a generous ice piece to the shaker and shake vigorously for 10–15 seconds.
3. Fill two serving glasses with fresh ice cubes to the top.
4. Strain the punch evenly between the glasses for a chilled pour.
5. Garnish both glasses with a fresh pineapple wedge on the rim.
6. Serve immediately and enjoy the tropical burst of flavor.

NUTRITIONAL VALUES (PER SERVING):

Calories: 140 | Protein: 0g | Carbs: 12g | Fat: 0g

Spiced Rum Hot Apple Cider

INGREDIENTS

2 cups apple cider
3 oz spiced rum
¼ tsp cinnamon
Orange peel (optional)
Cinnamon sticks for garnish

2
SERVINGS

05 MINS
PREP TIME

INSTRUCTIONS

1. Pour apple cider into the small saucepan and warm over low heat.
2. Add cinnamon and stir gently to infuse the flavor as it heats.
3. Once hot but not boiling, remove from the heat and add the spiced rum.
4. Divide the mixture evenly between two heatproof mugs or cups.
5. Add a strip of orange peel for brightness if using.
6. Garnish both mugs with a cinnamon stick and serve warm.

NUTRITIONAL VALUES (PER SERVING):

Calories: 130 | Protein: 0g | Carbs: 14g | Fat: 0g

Frozen Strawberry Rum Daiquiri

2
SERVINGS

05 MINS
PREP TIME

INGREDIENTS

1½ cups frozen strawberries

3 oz white rum

1 oz lime juice

1 tbsp honey or sweetener

½ cup ice

INSTRUCTIONS

1. Add frozen strawberries, white rum, lime juice, honey, and ice to a blender.
2. Blend on full power until the mixture is smooth and slushy.
3. Stop and scrape down the sides, then pulse again to achieve an even texture.
4. Taste and adjust the sweetness with honey or lime.
5. Pour the daiquiri into two chilled cocktail glasses.
6. Garnish with a lime slice or whole strawberry, and serve immediately.

NUTRITIONAL VALUES (PER SERVING):

Calories: 150 | Protein: 1g | Carbs: 15g | Fat: 0g

Mango Coconut Rum Colada

INGREDIENTS

1 cup frozen mango chunks
½ cup coconut milk
3 oz white rum
1 tbsp honey or sweetener
(optional)
½ cup ice
Mango slices or toasted
coconut for garnish

2
SERVINGS

05 MINS
PREP TIME

INSTRUCTIONS

1. Add mango chunks, coconut milk, rum, sweetener, and ice to a blender.
2. Blend until smooth and creamy with a thick, tropical texture.
3. Taste and adjust sweetness or thickness by adding more honey or coconut milk.
4. Ladle into two chilled glasses, filling to the top.
5. Garnish with mango pieces or a sprinkle of toasted coconut.
6. Serve immediately with a straw or spoon.

NUTRITIONAL VALUES (PER SERVING):

Calories: 160 | Protein: 1g | Carbs: 16g | Fat: 6g

Honey-Rum Old Fashioned

INGREDIENTS

2 oz dark rum
½ tsp honey
2 dashes Angostura bitters
1 tsp warm water
Orange peel for garnish
Ice cube (large)

2
SERVINGS

05 MINS
PREP TIME

INSTRUCTIONS

1. In a mixing glass, stir the honey with warm water until it is fully dissolved.
2. Add dark rum and bitters, then stir gently to combine.
3. Place a large ice cube in a short glass.
4. Strain the rum mixture over the ice.
5. Twist with an orange peel over the drink to release oils, then drop it in.
6. Let it sit for a moment, then sip slowly.

NUTRITIONAL VALUES (PER SERVING):

Calories: 120 | Protein: 0g | Carbs: 4g | Fat: 0g

Watermelon Basil Rum Cooler

INGREDIENTS

2 cups watermelon, cubed
4–5 fresh basil leaves
3 oz white rum
1 oz lime juice
Ice cubes
Sparkling water to top

2
SERVINGS

05 MINS
PREP TIME

INSTRUCTIONS

1. In a food blender, puree watermelon until smooth, then strain if preferred.
2. Gently crush basil leaves in each glass to release their aroma.
3. Add ice to the glasses and ladle in watermelon juice, rum, and lime juice.
4. Stir gently to combine the ingredients.
5. Top each glass with sparkling water to add a fizzy finish.
6. Garnish with a basil leaf and a small slice of watermelon.

NUTRITIONAL VALUES (PER SERVING):

Calories: 110 | Protein: 1g | Carbs: 10g | Fat: 0g

Cinnamon Spiced Rum Toddy

INGREDIENTS

2 oz spiced rum
1 tbsp honey
2 cups hot water
½ tsp ground cinnamon
2 lemon slices
Cinnamon sticks for garnish

2
SERVINGS

05 MINS
PREP TIME

INSTRUCTIONS

1. In a small pot, warm water over low heat and add honey until it is dissolved.
2. Add cinnamon and let it steep for 1–2 minutes.
3. Remove from heat and toss in the spiced rum.
4. Divide the liquid into two mugs.
5. Add a lemon slice to each cup for brightness.
6. Add a cinnamon stick, garnish, and serve hot.

NUTRITIONAL VALUES (PER SERVING):

Calories: 100 | Protein: 0g | Carbs: 6g | Fat: 0g

Blackberry Lime Rum Smash

INGREDIENTS

6–8 fresh blackberries
1 oz lime juice
2 oz dark rum
1 tsp honey or sweetener
Crushed ice
Fresh mint or lime wedge for garnish

2
SERVINGS

05 MINS
PREP TIME

INSTRUCTIONS

1. In a shaker or sturdy glass, muddle blackberries with lime juice and honey.
2. Add dark rum and fill the shaker with ice.
3. Shake vigorously for 13–15 seconds to chill and combine the ingredients.
4. Strain the drink into a short serving glass filled with crushed ice.
5. Garnish with mint or a lime wedge on the rim.
6. Serve with a short straw and enjoy the cold.

NUTRITIONAL VALUES (PER SERVING):

Calories: 130 | Protein: 0g | Carbs: 10g | Fat: 0g

www.ingramcontent.com/pod-product-compliance
Lightning Source LLC
Chambersburg PA
CBHW081003140626
46546CB00018B/3092